W9-BCT-401

Team Spirit

THE WASHINGTON NATIONALS

BY

MARK STEWART

Content Consultant
James L. Gates, Jr.
Library Director
National Baseball Hall of Fame and Museum

NORWOOD HOUSE PRESS

CHICAGO, ILLINOIS

Norwood House Press
P.O. Box 316598
Chicago, Illinois 60631

For information regarding Norwood House Press, please visit our website at:
www.norwoodhousepress.com or call 866-565-2900.

All photos courtesy of **Getty Images** except the following:
Topps, Inc. (7, 14, 17, 20, 22 top, 34 top right & bottom left, 36, 38, 40 top & bottom left, 43);
Black Book archives (18, 21 top, 22 bottom, 23 top, 37, 39, 41 left);
Author's collection (34 bottom right); O-Pee-Chee Ltd. (41 top); Matt Richman (48 top).
Page 12 photo courtesy of Washington Nationals.
Cover photo by Diamond Images/Getty Images.
Special thanks to Topps, Inc.

Editor: Mike Kennedy
Designer: Ron Jaffe
Project Management: Black Book Partners, LLC.
Special thanks to Thomas J. Doyle.

Library of Congress Cataloging-in-Publication Data

Stewart, Mark, 1960-
  The Washington Nationals / by Mark Stewart ; content consultant,
 James L.
Gates, Jr.
      p. cm. -- (Team spirit)
  Summary: "Presents the history, accomplishments and key personalities of
the Washington Nationals baseball team. Includes timelines, quotes, maps,
glossary and website"--Provided by publisher.
  Includes bibliographical references and index.
  ISBN-13: 978-1-59953-178-6 (library edition : alk. paper)
  ISBN-10: 1-59953-178-X (library edition : alk. paper) 1. Washington
Nationals (Baseball team)--History--Juvenile literature. I. Gates, James L.
II. Title.
GV863.W18.S74 2008
796.357'6409753--dc22
                                                    2007043503

3693

COVER PHOTO: The Nationals celebrate a game-winning home run during
the 2007 season.

Table of Contents

CHAPTER	PAGE
Meet the Nationals	4
Way Back When	6
The Team Today	10
Home Turf	12
Dressed for Success	14
We Won!	16
Go-To Guys	20
On the Sidelines	24
One Great Day	26
Legend Has It	28
It Really Happened	30
Team Spirit	32
Timeline	34
Fun Facts	36
Talking Baseball	38
For the Record	40
Pinpoints	42
Play Ball	44
Glossary	46
Places to Go	47
Index	48

SPORTS WORDS & VOCABULARY WORDS: In this book, you will find many words that are new to you. You may also see familiar words used in new ways. The glossary on page 46 gives the meanings of baseball words, as well as "everyday" words that have special baseball meanings. These words appear in **bold type** throughout the book. The glossary on page 47 gives the meanings of vocabulary words that are not related to baseball. They appear in ***bold italic type*** throughout the book.

Meet the Nationals

Winning a baseball game is not an easy thing to do. It takes nine players at their very best to deliver the pitching, defense, smart baserunning, and **clutch hitting** needed for a victory. To perform consistently over the course of a full season, a team must keep great focus every game. The Washington Nationals have shown that they have these abilities.

The team first learned the lessons of baseball as the Montreal Expos. The Expos had good players and won a lot of games. They were an exciting team that did not make a lot of mistakes. The Expos were a joy to watch.

This book tells the story of the Nationals. They started in a city in Canada and moved to the capital of the United States. Fans of the Nationals root for their team with all their heart. Washington's players are dedicated to giving those fans a winner.

The Nationals celebrate a home run during the 2007 season.
On the field, they feed off the enthusiasm shown by their fans.

Way Back When

Baseball in Washington, D.C. has a long and unusual history. The city had a **National League (NL)** team in the 1800s, and from 1901 to 1971, two different **American League (AL)** teams played there. So it's no surprise that the city's current team, the Nationals, actually moved to Washington from another country!

In 1969, the NL added two new teams. One was the San Diego Padres, and the other was the Expos, who played in Montreal,

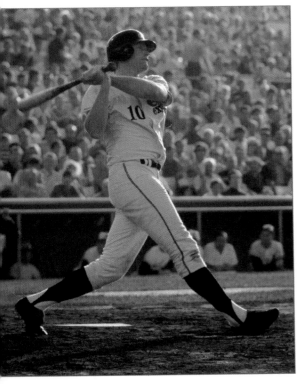

Canada. Two years earlier, Montreal had held a successful World's Fair called Expo 67. The city would also host the Summer Olympics in 1976. Montreal was truly an *international* city, and **Major League Baseball** was excited about the idea of bringing the game to a worldwide audience.

The Expos put good players on the field right away. Their stars included Bill Stoneman, Rusty Staub, Mack Jones, and Steve Renko. Just a few games into the 1969 season, Stoneman pitched a **no-hitter** against the Philadelphia Phillies. Over the next few years, many more good players wore the Montreal uniform, including Mike Torrez, Mike Marshall, Ken Singleton, and Ron Hunt.

STEVE ROGERS

By the late 1970s, the Expos had *assembled* a very talented team. Catcher Gary Carter, third baseman Larry Parrish, and outfielders Warren Cromartie, Ellis Valentine, and Andre Dawson formed the heart of the batting order. During the early 1980s, Montreal developed an excellent **pitching staff** led by Steve Rogers, Scott Sanderson, Bill Gullickson, Charlie Lea, and Jeff Reardon.

Montreal welcomed many other star players, including Tim Raines, Tim Wallach, Andres Galarraga, and Dennis Martinez. Despite all of this talent, however, the team had a hard time winning more often than it lost. Montreal made the **playoffs** just once, in 1981. The team won a playoff series against the Phillies but then lost the **National League Championship Series (NLCS)** to the Los Angeles Dodgers.

LEFT: Rusty Staub, one of Montreal's first stars.
ABOVE: Steve Rogers, the team's best pitcher from 1973 to 1983.

7

The Expos rose again in the 1990s. Those teams were paced by outfielders Larry Walker, Moises Alou, and Marquis Grissom, and pitchers Pedro Martinez, Ken Hill, and John Wetteland. In 1994, Montreal had the best team in baseball. The Expos seemed headed to the **World Series** until the season ended in August over a labor dispute.

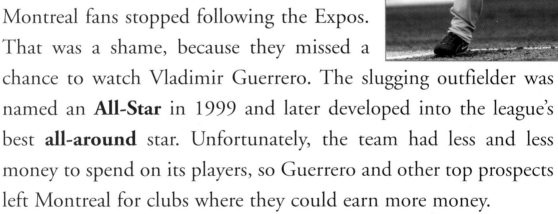

Heartbroken and *frustrated*, many Montreal fans stopped following the Expos. That was a shame, because they missed a chance to watch Vladimir Guerrero. The slugging outfielder was named an **All-Star** in 1999 and later developed into the league's best **all-around** star. Unfortunately, the team had less and less money to spend on its players, so Guerrero and other top prospects left Montreal for clubs where they could earn more money.

In 2002, Major League Baseball took over the Expos, because the team was losing too much money to stay in business. In 2005, the club moved to Washington, D.C. and was renamed the Nationals. Fans there were overjoyed. The Nationals began putting together the building blocks of a championship team.

LEFT: Pedro Martinez, the leader of Montreal's pitching staff in the 1990s.
ABOVE: Vladimir Guerrero waits for his pitch.

The Team Today

Many baseball fans wondered how the Expos would change when they moved to Washington. Would the newly named Nationals sign big-name players to lure big crowds to the ballpark? Would the team *invest* in young players and ask the fans to be *patient*?

The Nationals ended up doing a little bit of both. They found *experienced* hitters such as Vinny Castilla, Jose Guillen, Alfonso Soriano, and Dmitri Young. But the team also slowly worked in young players such as Ryan Zimmerman, Chad Cordero, Lastings Milledge, Nick Johnson, Brad Wilkerson, and Ryan Church.

Now the team's future is in the hands of its up-and-coming stars. The fans are excited about where the team is headed. The Nationals know that finding the right combination of youth and experience is all you need to have a winning season.

Ryan Zimmerman is congratulated by teammates after a big win. The Nationals work to build a winning team around young stars such as Zimmerman.

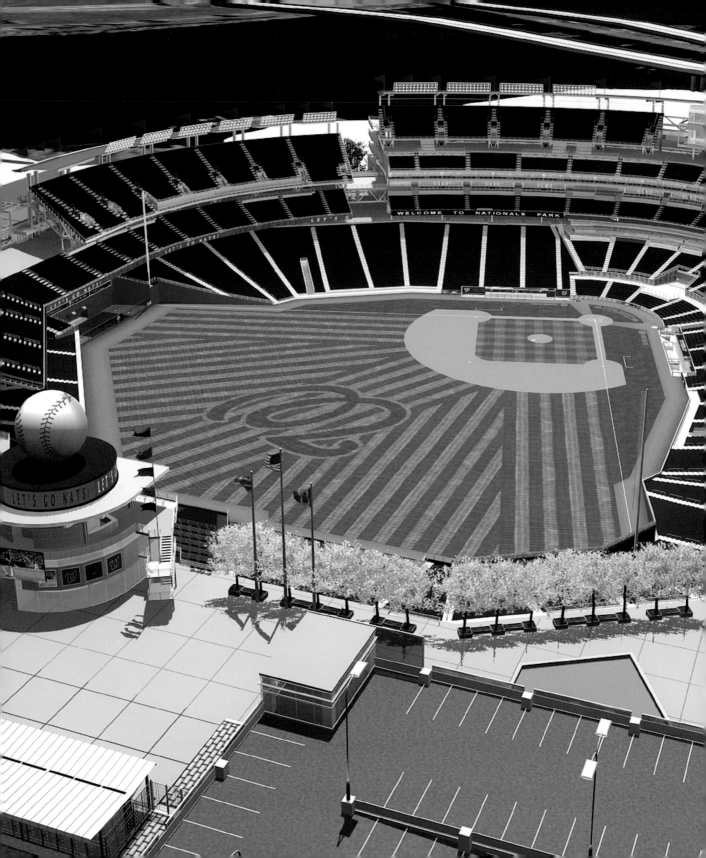

Home Turf

When the team played its first game as the Expos, its home was Jarry Park Stadium in Montreal. Many fans remember home runs splashing into a city swimming pool beyond the right field fence. In 1977, the Expos moved into Olympic Stadium, which was built for the 1976 *Summer Olympics*.

When the Nationals moved into their new home in Washington, it was actually an old home. Robert F. Kennedy Memorial Stadium (also known as RFK Stadium) had been the ballpark of the Washington Senators before they moved away in 1972. The Nationals played three seasons at RFK while a new stadium was built. Nationals Park opened for the 2008 season.

BY THE NUMBERS

- *The Nationals' stadium has 41,222 seats.*
- *The distance from home plate to the left field foul pole is 335 feet.*
- *The distance from home plate to the center field fence is 408 feet.*
- *The distance from home plate to the right field foul pole is 335 feet.*
- *The Nationals were 122–121 during their three years in RFK Stadium.*

A colorful picture shows the Nationals' new stadium, which opened for the 2008 season.

Dressed for Success

The Expos had a very "mod-looking" *logo* when they first took the field in 1969. The red, white, and blue *M* on their caps was actually a combination of three letters—*EMB*. Those letters stood for "Expos de Montréal Baseball," the team's name in French. The Expos used that *M* and the team colors for all 35 seasons they played in Canada.

The Nationals kept those team colors. They also added touches of gold. The Nationals like to use many different color combinations in their uniforms. Some are very modern. Others are historic. For most games, however, red has been the main uniform color.

The team's logo includes nine stars, which stand for the nine positions on a baseball field. The logo also spells out the team's name in capital letters. At times, the Nationals pay tribute to their city's baseball past. For example, they sometimes wear the old caps of the Washington Senators.

A trading card shows Tim Foli in Montreal's red, white, and blue uniform from the mid-1970s.

14

The baseball uniform has not changed much since the Nationals began playing. It has four main parts:

- a cap or batting helmet with a sun visor
- a top with a player's number on the back
- pants that reach down between the ankle and the knee
- stirrup-style socks

The uniform top sometimes has a player's name on the back. The team's name, city, or logo is usually on the front. Baseball teams wear light-colored uniforms when they play at home and darker styles when they play on the road.

For more than 100 years, baseball uniforms were made of wool *flannel* and were very baggy. This helped the sweat *evaporate* and gave players the freedom to move around. Today's uniforms are made of *synthetic* fabrics that stretch with players and keep them dry and cool.

Dmitri Young wears one of Washington's 2007 home uniforms.

We Won!

The Montreal Expos began building a strong *core* of talent in their early years. By the end of the 1970s, they had one of the best teams in baseball. The Expos came very close to winning the **NL East** in 1979 and 1980. Both times they were beaten out in the final weekend of the season, first by the Pittsburgh Pirates and then by the Philadelphia Phillies. In 1981, the Expos were 30–25 and in third place when a baseball strike *interrupted* the season. The strike lasted more than seven weeks.

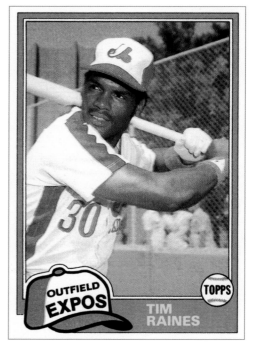

LEFT: Gary Carter tags out a runner at home plate during the 1981 season.
RIGHT: Tim Raines, Montreal's great rookie that year.

Montreal fans could hardly wait for the season to restart. Their team was led by young **sluggers** Gary Carter and Andre Dawson. The Expos also had a speedy **rookie** named Tim Raines. He batted over .300 and could steal a base almost any time he wanted.

Montreal's pitching was excellent, too. Steve Rogers and Bill Gullickson were two of the best **starters** in the league. A year earlier, Gullickson had struck out 18 batters in a game. The team's **bullpen** was solid as well. During the season, the Expos had traded for hard-throwing Jeff Reardon. He **saved** six games and posted a 1.30 **earned run average (ERA)** the rest of the way.

When the season resumed, it was announced that every team's record would start at 0–0. The first-place team from the first half of the season would play the first-place team from the second half. The Expos played well and finished one game ahead of the St. Louis Cardinals. They faced the Phillies for the NL East championship. The first team to win three games would move on to the NLCS and play for the **pennant**.

The Expos took the first two games, each by a score of 3–1. Rogers and Gullickson were brilliant, and Reardon saved both games. The Phillies did not give up easily. They had won the 1980 World Series and wanted a chance to repeat as champions. Philadelphia won the next game 6–2 and then tied the series with a 6–5 victory in extra innings in Game Four.

Rogers faced Philadelphia's top pitcher, Steve Carlton, in the final game. The Expos loaded the bases in the fifth inning, and Rogers came to bat. He shocked Carlton and the Phillies by hitting a single. Larry Parrish and Chris Speier scored to make the score 2–0. Parrish drove in another run one inning later.

ABOVE: Andre Dawson, the team's most dangerous hitter in 1981.
RIGHT: Steve Rogers looks to home plate as he winds up for a pitch.

Rogers pitched all nine innings and allowed just six hits and no runs. The last out of the game came on a line drive that was caught by first baseman Warren Cromartie. The Expos were division champions!

Sadly for Montreal fans, the team fell short of winning the pennant. They matched up against the Los Angeles Dodgers in the NLCS and lost three games to two. Game Five was a tense battle that Los Angeles won 2–1 on a run in the ninth inning. When the Expos left Montreal and became the Nationals 24 years later, the team still had not played in a World Series.

Go-To Guys

To be a true star in baseball, you need more than a quick bat and a strong arm. You have to be a "go-to guy"—someone the manager wants on the pitcher's mound or in the batter's box when it matters most. Fans of the Expos and the Nationals have had a lot to cheer about over the years, including these great stars …

THE PIONEERS

STEVE ROGERS   Pitcher

• BORN: 10/26/1949   • PLAYED FOR TEAM: 1973 TO 1985
When the Expos needed a victory, they handed the ball to Steve Rogers. He led the NL in **shutouts** twice and ERA once, and almost never missed a start. Rogers had an unusual style. He seemed to stumble after delivering every pitch.

GARY CARTER   Catcher

• BORN: 4/8/1954   • PLAYED FOR TEAM: 1974 TO 1984 & 1992
Gary Carter was an excellent defensive catcher and a great team leader. He was an All-Star almost every year and an *extraordinary* clutch hitter. Carter was the first Expo elected to the **Hall of Fame**.

ABOVE: Gary Carter
TOP RIGHT: Andre Dawson   **BOTTOM RIGHT**: Tim Wallach

ANDRE DAWSON   Outfielder

- BORN: 7/10/1954
- PLAYED FOR TEAM: 1976 TO 1986

Andre Dawson was nicknamed the "Hawk" for the way he hunted down deep drives in the outfield. He could also hit the ball a long way. Dawson was the only player to slam 200 home runs and steal 200 bases in an Expos uniform.

TIM RAINES   Outfielder

- BORN: 9/16/1959
- PLAYED FOR TEAM: 1979 TO 1990 & 2001

Tim Raines was the most exciting player on the Expos during the 1980s. He stole at least 70 bases six years in a row and was the NL batting champion in 1986.

TIM WALLACH   Third Baseman

- BORN: 9/14/1957
- PLAYED FOR TEAM: 1980 TO 1992

Tim Wallach came to the team after winning the Golden Spikes Award as America's best college baseball player. He was an All-Star five times for the Expos and won three **Gold Glove** awards for his excellent fielding. Wallach also led the NL in doubles twice.

JEFF REARDON
Pitcher

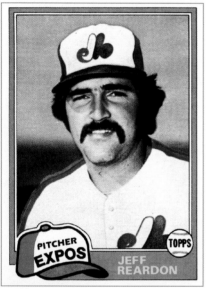

- BORN: 10/1/1955 • PLAYED FOR TEAM: 1981 TO 1986

Jeff Reardon was a true "stopper." The team usually left him in the bullpen until the ninth inning so he could come in and stop an opponent's threat. Reardon recorded 152 saves in a Montreal uniform.

DENNIS MARTINEZ
Pitcher

- BORN: 5/14/1955 • PLAYED FOR TEAM: 1986 TO 1993

Dennis Martinez was the first big leaguer from the country of Nicaragua. He had many different pitches, and batters rarely got good swings against him. In 1991, Martinez threw a perfect game—27 batters, 27 outs—against the Los Angeles Dodgers.

PEDRO MARTINEZ
Pitcher

- BORN: 10/25/1971 • PLAYED FOR TEAM: 1994 TO 1997

Before Pedro Martinez was a star with the Boston Red Sox and New York Mets, he was the top pitcher on the Expos. He joined the team as a hard-throwing **relief pitcher** but soon became the NL's top starter. Martinez won the **Cy Young Award** in 1997.

VLADIMIR GUERRERO   Outfielder

- BORN: 2/9/1976   • PLAYED FOR TEAM: 1996 TO 2003

Vladimir Guerrero was one of the most talented and confident players the team ever had. No Montreal fan ever left the ballpark if he was due to bat one more time. Guerrero believed he could hit any pitch over the fence or throw out any baserunner—and he often did!

JOSE VIDRO   Second Baseman

- BORN: 8/27/1974   • PLAYED FOR TEAM: 1997 TO 2006

Jose Vidro hit the ball hard and almost never struck out. Vidro's batting average during his years with the team was better than .300.

RYAN ZIMMERMAN   Third Baseman

- BORN: 9/28/1984   • FIRST YEAR WITH TEAM: 2005

Few young players have ever fielded and hit better than Ryan Zimmerman. He made amazing plays at third base and became known for hitting **walk-off homers** to win games. Many compared Zimmerman to Hall of Famer Brooks Robinson at the same age.

TOP LEFT: Jeff Reardon   **BOTTOM LEFT**: Pedro Martinez
TOP RIGHT: Vladimir Guerrero   **BOTTOM RIGHT**: Ryan Zimmerman

On the Sidelines

When the Nationals began their first season in Washington, their manager was Frank Robinson. He was the right man for the job. Robinson **demanded** hustle and effort from his players, but he was also a patient teacher.

Before Robinson, the Expos had other top managers. Their first skipper, Gene Mauch, turned a group of **castoffs** into a contender in just a few years. The Expos took their next big step forward under Dick Williams. He was a tough, smart manager who made good players great. During his time in the dugout, the Expos had one of the best teams in baseball.

During the 1980s and 1990s, the team was led by Buck Rodgers and Felipe Alou. They were two of the sport's most respected managers. In 2007, the Nationals hired Manny Acta to run the club. He had been a coach for the Expos and the New York Mets. Acta also managed the Dominican Republic team that played in baseball tournaments around the world.

Frank Robinson smiles for the camera during his days as the manager of the Nationals.

One Great Day

When Pedro Martinez was a young Expo, his teammates predicted that one day he would be unhittable. They were right. As an up-and-coming star in 1994, Martinez nearly threw a no-hitter—in just the fifth start of his career! One year later, in a June game against the Padres in San Diego, he was at it again. Martinez had all of his pitches working. The poor Padres could barely touch the ball.

San Diego was not a weak-hitting team. The team's **lineup** included sluggers Ken Caminiti and Steve Finley, as well as batting champion Tony Gwynn. But on this day, Martinez was in full command. Up the Padres came to the plate and down they went for nine innings.

Martinez did not allow a hit or a walk to the first 27 San Diego batters. Normally, this would have been a perfect game. However, Joey Hamilton of the Padres was pitching great, too. He allowed just three hits and had not surrendered a run, either. After nine innings, the score was tied 0–0.

In the top of the 10th inning, Montreal finally scored, when Jeff Treadway drove in Shane Andrews for the game's only run. Martinez

Pedro Martinez during his attempt at a perfect game against the San Diego Padres.

came out to start the bottom of the 10th. The first batter, Bip Roberts, lined a pitch to center field. Tony Tarasco tried to catch the ball but could not reach it before it bounced on the outfield grass. The perfect game and no-hitter were lost.

There was still a game to be won, however. Manager Felipe Alou decided to take out his young starter. Mel Rojas replaced Martinez and retired the next three Padres for a 1–0 victory. Afterward, all anyone could talk about was the incredible nine innings thrown by Martinez.

Legend Has It

Who was the first player to hit a ball out of a domed stadium?

LEGEND HAS IT that Montreal outfielder Rondell White was. In 1998, the Expos decided to make changes to the roof that covered Olympic Stadium. This created a small gap in the stands down the left field line. White hit a long ball that was just foul—but flew entirely out of the stadium!

ABOVE: Rondell White
RIGHT: Ken Singleton in his double-knit uniform.

Why did baseball teams switch from flannel uniforms to synthetic fabrics?

LEGEND HAS IT that the Expos started the idea. One of their star players, Ken Singleton, was *allergic* to the wool in the team's flannel uniform. The team started using a style called double-knit. It was stretchy and colorful, and not baggy like the old uniforms. All the players loved it. By the end of 1973, every team in the big leagues had decided to switch to the new material.

Who had the best team in baseball in 1994?

LEGEND HAS IT that the Expos did. The stars of the 1994 team included Moises Alou, Larry Walker, Marquis Grissom, Wil Cordero, Ken Hill, and John Wetteland. On August 11th, Montreal's record was 74–40. The Expos were the only team in baseball with more than 70 victories. It looked as if Montreal might win its first championship, but an argument between baseball's owners and players stopped the season. They did not settle their differences in time to play the World Series, so the Expos never had the chance to prove how good they really were.

It Really Happened

When Greg Harris joined the Expos in 1995, he was nearing the end of his pitching career. He had been in the major leagues since 1981. During that time, he had worn the uniforms of eight different teams. Harris was a good pitcher but never a star. He did not think he would ever be elected to the Hall of Fame.

Before he retired, Harris had a trick up his sleeve. He was ambidextrous—which meant that he could pitch left-handed and right-handed. Though Harris had thrown as a righty for his entire life, he had spent many years practicing as a lefty, too. Harris had one wish. He wanted to pitch from both sides in a big-league game. On September 28th of the 1995 season, the Expos allowed him to do it.

Harris came into a game against the Cincinnati Reds wearing a special glove that could be worn on either hand. The glove had a thumb at both ends and four finger slots in between them. The first batter Harris faced was righty Reggie Sanders. Harris pitched to him right-handed and got him out. The next batter was lefty Hal Morris. Harris pitched to him left-handed and walked him.

Harris throws a pitch as a right-hander.

Harris pitched left-handed to the next hitter, Eddie Taubensee, also a lefty. Taubensee grounded out. Harris then switched back to right-handed pitching to retire the final batter of the inning, righty Bret Boone.

The last player to pitch both right-handed and left-handed in a game was Elton Chamberlain, in 1888. In those days, many pitchers did not wear gloves, so it was easier to switch back and forth. Harris accomplished the feat the hard way.

While Harris never made it to the Hall of Fame, the glove he used on that historic day did. It is there today so fans can always remember that special moment.

Team Spirit

In the 1960s, baseball in Montreal seemed to have a bright future. Unfortunately, by the end of the 1990s, the Expos could not afford to compete with the other teams in the NL. The club would have to leave Montreal.

In Washington, D.C., the newly named Nationals found millions of fans who supported them with tremendous passion. A look at the stadium parking lot shows license plates from Virginia, Maryland, Delaware, West Virginia, and North Carolina. During their first season in Washington, the Nationals welcomed nearly three million fans to the ballpark.

One of their favorite things to do at Nationals games is watch Screech, the team's *mascot*. Screech is a young eagle who moves all over the stadium. Sometimes he arrives in the red, white, and blue Screech Mobile. All the time, he makes the fans laugh.

Screech likes to get the crowd excited with performances on top of the dugout.

Timeline

Bill
Stoneman

1972
Bill Stoneman
pitches his second
no-hitter as an Expo.

1978
Ross Grimsley becomes the
team's first 20-game winner.

1969
The team plays its
first season as the
Montreal Expos.

1974
Bad weather causes the Expos
to play 24 **doubleheaders**
during the season.

1985
Andre Dawson wins
his sixth Gold Glove
in a row.

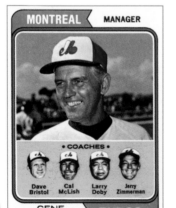

Gene Mauch,
Montreal's first
manager.

A souvenir
pennant from
the team's
early days.

Delino
DeShields

1990
Delino DeShields
gets four hits in his
first big-league game.

2005
The team moves to Washington,
D.C. and is renamed the Nationals.

1997
Mark Grudzielanek
leads the NL with
54 doubles.

2003
Jose Vidro starts in
the All-Star Game
for the second time.

2006
Alfonso Soriano is the first player to
hit 40 doubles and 40 homers and
steal 40 bases in the same season.

Mark
Grudzielanek

Alfonso Soriano
holds the 40th
base he stole
in 2006.

Fun Facts

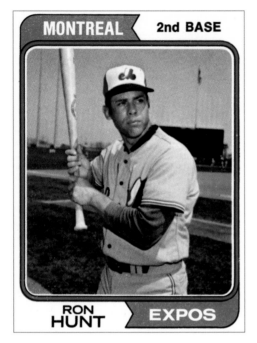

MONTREAL · 2nd BASE

RON HUNT · EXPOS

OUCH!

In 1971, Ron Hunt set a record when he was hit by a pitch 50 times.

WHO'S ON THIRD?

Rodney Scott stole third base 24 times during the 1980 season. Only two other Montreal players stole second base more times than that during the year.

GIANT KILLER

Charlie Lea pitched a no-hitter against the San Francisco Giants in May 1981. In his next game, he shut out the Giants on four hits.

GOOD COMPANY

In 2006, Ryan Zimmerman became just the third NL rookie in the last 50 years to reach 100 **runs batted in (RBI)** in one season. The other two were All-Stars Mike Piazza and Albert Pujols.

ABOVE: Ron Hunt
RIGHT: Felipe Alou, with his son, Moises, in the background.

ROAD WARRIORS

In 1991, a damaged beam made Montreal's stadium unsafe for fans, so the Expos had to play their home games in the other teams' ballparks. Montreal took the field for 93 games on the road. Normally, a team plays 81 games at home and 81 games away from home.

FATHER-SON GAME

In 1992, Felipe Alou managed his son, Moises. It was only the fifth time in history that had happened.

BIG MACK

On April 14, 1969, Mack Jones hit a **grand slam** in Montreal's first home game. It was the first major-league home run hit outside the United States.

LEADOFF MAN

The first batter in team history was Maury Wills. The Expos traded him to the Los Angeles Dodgers two months later.

Talking Baseball

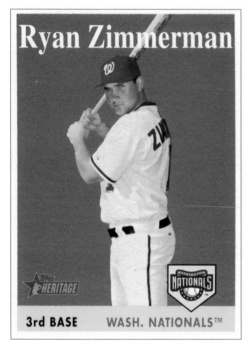

Ryan Zimmerman

3rd BASE   WASH. NATIONALS™

"When I was younger, I was always smaller. I couldn't hit, so I had to work on defense."

—Ryan Zimmerman, on how he became a great fielder

"It is a **grueling** position. My knees will tell you that!"

—Gary Carter, on the hardships of catching

"I love my teammates, and I'll do anything for them."

—Pedro Martinez, on his baseball friendships

"A lot of the kids are not having the same advantage I had when I was growing up—playing baseball."

—Manny Acta, on why he is building a baseball complex in his hometown in the Dominican Republic

ABOVE: Ryan Zimmerman
RIGHT: Larry Walker

"The fun feeling you get playing keeps your head up when you encounter difficult times."

> —*Vladimir Guerrero, on what baseball meant to him as a boy*

"I'm not the manager because I'm always right. I'm always right because I'm the manager!"

> —*Gene Mauch, on being in charge of a baseball team*

"You can't steal bases if you don't get on base. It's all about getting opportunities, and every time you get on base you're giving your team an opportunity to score."

> —*Tim Raines, on what made him a great player*

"Baseball is not a game played on paper."

> —*Larry Walker, on why the underdog always has a chance to win*

For the Record

T he great Expos and Nationals teams and players have left their marks on the record books. These are the "best of the best" …

Andre Dawson

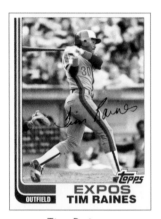

Tim Raines

NATIONALS AWARD WINNERS

WINNER	AWARD	YEAR
Carl Morton	Rookie of the Year*	1970
Gene Mauch	Manager of the Year	1973
Andre Dawson	Rookie of the Year	1977
Dick Williams	Manager of the Year	1979
Gary Carter	All-Star Game MVP	1981
Gary Carter	All-Star Game MVP	1984
Tim Raines	All-Star Game MVP	1987
Buck Rodgers	Manager of the Year	1987
Felipe Alou	Manager of the Year	1994
Pedro Martinez	Cy Young Award	1997
Dmitri Young	Comeback Player of the Year	2007

The annual award given to each league's best first-year player.

Gary
Carter

NATIONALS ACHIEVEMENTS

ACHIEVEMENT	YEAR
NL East Second-Half Champions*	1981
NL East Champions	1981
NL East Champions	1994

The 1981 season was played with first-half and second-half division winners.

Montreal Expos
outfield **ELLIS VALENTINE** voltigeur
Card Number 7 of 24 - Carte Numéro 7 de 24
© 1981 O-Pee-Chee Co. Ltd. Printed in Canada - Imprimé au Canada

DICK WILLIAMS
Gérant/Manager

TOP: Ellis Valentine, a leader on the 1981 team.
ABOVE: Dick Williams, the 1979 Manager of the Year.
LEFT: Moises Alou, a star on the 1994 club.

41

Pinpoints

T he history of a baseball team is made up of many smaller stories. These stories take place all over the map—not just in the city a team calls "home." Match the pushpins on these maps to the Team Facts and you will begin to see the story of the Nationals unfold!

TEAM FACTS

1   Washington, D.C.—*The team has played here since 2005.*

2   Washington, North Carolina—*Ryan Zimmerman was born here.*

3   Atlanta, Georgia—*Mack Jones was born here.*

4   Sanford, Florida—*Tim Raines was born here.*

5   Jefferson City, Missouri—*Steve Rogers was born here.*

6   Helena, Arkansas—*Ellis Valentine was born here.*

7   Oak Park, Illinois—*Bill Stoneman was born here.*

8   Upland, California—*Chad Cordero was born here.*

9   Culver City, California—*Gary Carter was born here.*

10   Montreal, Quebec, Canada—*The team played here as the Expos from 1969 to 2004.*

11   Granada, Nicaragua—*Dennis Martinez was born here.*

12   Nizao, Dominican Republic—*Vladimir Guerrero was born here.*

Chad Cordero

Play Ball

Baseball is a game played between two teams over nine innings. Teams take one turn at bat and one turn in the field during each inning. A turn at bat ends when three outs are made. The batters on the hitting team try to reach base safely. The players on the fielding team try to prevent this from happening.

In baseball, the ball is controlled by the pitcher. The pitcher must throw the ball to the batter, who decides whether or not to swing at each pitch. If a batter swings and misses, it is a strike. If the batter lets a good pitch go by, it is also a strike. If the batter swings and the ball does not stay in fair territory (between the v-shaped lines that begin at home plate) it is called "foul," and is counted as a strike. If the pitcher throws three strikes, the batter is out. If the pitcher throws four bad pitches before that, the batter is awarded first base. This is called a base-on-balls, or "walk."

When the batter swings the bat and hits the ball, everyone springs into action. If a fielder catches a batted ball before it hits the ground, the batter is out. If a fielder scoops the ball off the ground and throws it to first base before the batter arrives, the batter is out. If the batter reaches first base safely, he is credited with a hit. A one-base hit is called a single, a two-base hit is called a double, a three-base hit is called a triple, and a four-base hit is called a home run.

Runners who reach base are only safe when they are touching one of the bases. If they are caught between the bases, the fielders can tag them with the ball and record an out.

A batter who is able to circle the bases and make it back to home plate before three outs are made is credited with a run scored. The team with the most runs after nine innings is the winner.

Anyone who has played baseball (or softball) knows that it can be a complicated game. Every player on the field has a job to do. Different players have different strengths and weaknesses. The pitchers, batters, and managers make hundreds of decisions every game. The more you play and watch baseball, the more "little things" you are likely to notice. The next time you are at a game, look for these plays:

PLAY LIST

DOUBLE PLAY—A play where the fielding team is able to make two outs on one batted ball. This usually happens when a runner is on first base, and the batter hits a ground ball to one of the infielders. The base runner is forced out at second base and the ball is then thrown to first base before the batter arrives.

HIT AND RUN—A play where the runner on first base sprints to second base while the pitcher is throwing the ball to the batter. When the second baseman or shortstop moves toward the base to wait for the catcher's throw, the batter tries to hit the ball to the place that the fielder has just left. If the batter swings and misses, the fielding team can tag the runner out.

INTENTIONAL WALK—A play when the pitcher throws four bad pitches on purpose, allowing the batter to walk to first base. This happens when the pitcher would much rather face the next batter—and is willing to risk putting a runner on base.

SACRIFICE BUNT—A play where the batter makes an out on purpose so that a teammate can move to the next base. On a bunt, the batter tries to "deaden" the pitch with the bat instead of swinging at it.

SHOESTRING CATCH—A play where an outfielder catches a short hit an inch or two above the ground, near the tops of his shoes. It is not easy to run as fast as you can and lower your glove without slowing down. It can be risky, too. If a fielder misses a shoestring catch, the ball might roll all the way to the fence.

Glossary

BASEBALL WORDS TO KNOW

ALL-AROUND—Good at all parts of the game.

ALL-STAR—A player who is selected to play in baseball's annual All-Star Game.

AMERICAN LEAGUE (AL)—One of baseball's two major leagues; the AL began play in 1901.

BULLPEN—The area where a team's relief pitchers warm up; this word also describes the group of relief pitchers in this area.

CLUTCH HITTING—Hitting well under pressure, or "in the clutch."

CY YOUNG AWARD—The annual trophy given to each league's best pitcher.

DOUBLEHEADERS—Series of games in which two games are scheduled to be played in one day.

EARNED RUN AVERAGE (ERA)—A statistic that counts how many runs a pitcher gives up for every nine innings he pitches.

GOLD GLOVE—An award given each year to baseball's best fielders.

GRAND SLAM—A home run with the bases loaded.

HALL OF FAME—The museum in Cooperstown, New York, where baseball's greatest players are honored. A player voted into the Hall of Fame is sometimes called a "Hall of Famer."

LINEUP—The list of players who are playing in a game.

MAJOR LEAGUE BASEBALL—The top level of professional baseball leagues. The American League and National League make up today's major leagues. Sometimes called the "big leagues."

NATIONAL LEAGUE (NL)—The older of the two major leagues; the NL began play in 1876.

NATIONAL LEAGUE CHAMPIONSHIP SERIES (NLCS)—The competition that has decided the National League pennant since 1969.

NL EAST—A group of National League teams that plays in the eastern part of the country.

NO-HITTER—A game in which a team is unable to get a hit.

PENNANT—A league championship. The term comes from the triangular flag awarded to each season's champion, beginning in the 1870s.

PITCHING STAFF—The group of players who pitch for a team.

PLAYOFFS—The games played after the regular season to determine which teams will advance to the World Series.

RELIEF PITCHER—A pitcher who is brought into a game to replace another pitcher. Relief pitchers can be seen warming up in the bullpen.

ROOKIE—A player in his first season.

RUNS BATTED IN (RBI)—A statistic that counts the number of runners a batter drives home.

SAVED—Recorded the last out in a team's win. A pitcher on the mound for the last out of a close victory is credited with a "save."

SHUTOUTS—Games in which one team does not allow its opponent to score a run.

SLUGGERS—Powerful hitters.

STARTERS—Pitchers who begin the game for their team.

WALK-OFF HOMERS—Home runs that win a game in the bottom of the final inning.

WORLD SERIES—The world championship series played between the winners of the National League and American League.

OTHER WORDS TO KNOW

ALLERGIC—Having a bodily reaction that causes sickness.

ASSEMBLED—Put together.

CASTOFFS—Unwanted people who are set adrift.

CORE—The central part of something.

DEMANDED—Asked for with authority.

EVAPORATE—Disappear, or turn into vapor.

EXPERIENCED—Having knowledge and skill in a job.

EXTRAORDINARY—Unusual or remarkable.

FLANNEL—A soft wool or cotton material.

FRUSTRATED—Disappointed and puzzled.

GRUELING—Exhausting.

INTERNATIONAL—From all over the world.

INTERRUPTED—Stopped or hindered.

INVEST—Spend money for the purpose of making money.

LOGO—A symbol or design that represents a company or team.

MASCOT—An animal or person believed to bring a group good luck.

PATIENT—Able to wait calmly.

SUMMER OLYMPICS—The warm-weather competition of the Olympics.

SYNTHETIC—Made in a laboratory, not in nature.

Places to Go

ON THE ROAD

WASHINGTON NATIONALS
1500 South Capitol Street Southeast
Washington, D.C. 20003
(202) 675-5100

**NATIONAL BASEBALL
HALL OF FAME AND MUSEUM**
25 Main Street
Cooperstown, New York 13326
(888) 425-5633
www.baseballhalloffame.org

ON THE WEB

THE WASHINGTON NATIONALS   www.nationals.com
  • *Learn more about the Nationals*

MAJOR LEAGUE BASEBALL   www.mlb.com
  • *Learn more about all the major league teams*

MINOR LEAGUE BASEBALL   www.minorleaguebaseball.com
  • *Learn more about the minor leagues*

ON THE BOOKSHELF

To learn more about the sport of baseball, look for these books at your library or bookstore:

  • Kelly, James. *Baseball*. New York, New York: DK, 2005.

  • Jacobs, Greg. *The Everything Kids' Baseball Book*. Cincinnati, Ohio:
    Adams Media Corporation, 2006.

  • Stewart, Mark and Kennedy, Mike. *Long Ball: The Legend and Lore of the Home Run*.
    Minneapolis, Minnesota: Millbrook Press, 2006.

47

Index

PAGE NUMBERS IN **BOLD** REFER TO ILLUSTRATIONS.

Acta, Manny	25, 38	Morris, Hal	30
Alou, Felipe	25, 27, 37, **37**, 40	Morton, Carl	40
Alou, Moises	9, 29, 37, **37**, **41**	Nationals Park	**12**, 13
Andrews, Shane	26	Olympic Stadium	13
Boone, Bret	31	Parrish, Larry	7, 18
Caminiti, Ken	26	Piazza, Mike	36
Carlton, Steve	18	Pujols, Albert	36
Carter, Gary	7, 16, **16**, 20,	Raines, Tim	7, 17, **17**, 21,
	20, 38, 40, **40**, 43		39, 40, **40**, 43
Castilla, Vinny	11	Reardon, Jeff	7, 17, 18, 22, **22**
Chamberlain, Elton	31	Renko, Steve	6
Church, Ryan	11	RFK Stadium	13
Cordero, Chad	11, 43, **43**	Roberts, Bip	27
Cordero, Wil	29	Robinson, Brooks	23
Cromartie, Warren	7, 19	Robinson, Frank	**24**, 25
Dawson, Andre	7, 17, 18, **18**,	Rodgers, Buck	25, 40
	21, **21**, 34, 40, **40**	Rogers, Steve	7, **7**, 17, 18,
DeShields, Delino	35, **35**		19, **19**, 20, 43
Finley, Steve	26	Rojas, Mel	27
Foli, Tim	**14**	Sanders, Reggie	30
Galarraga, Andres	7	Sanderson, Scott	7
Grimsley, Ross	34	Scott, Rodney	36
Grissom, Marquis	9, 29	Singleton, Ken	7, 29, **29**
Grudzielanek, Mark	35, **35**	Soriano, Alfonso	11, 35, **35**
Guerrero, Vladimir	9, **9**, 23,	Speier, Chris	18
	23, 39, 43	Staub, Rusty	6, **6**
Guillen, Jose	11	Stoneman, Bill	6, 7, 34, **34**, 43
Gullickson, Bill	7, 17, 18	Tarasco, Tony	27
Gwynn, Tony	26	Taubensee, Eddie	31
Hamilton, Joey	26	Torrez, Mike	7
Harris, Greg	30, 31, **31**	Treadway, Jeff	26
Hill, Ken	9, 29	Valentine, Ellis	7, **41**, 43
Hunt, Ron	7, 36, **36**	Vidro, Jose	23, 35
Jarry Park	13	Walker, Larry	9, 29, 39, **39**
Johnson, Nick	11	Wallach, Tim	7, 21, **21**
Jones, Mack	6, 37, 43	Wetteland, John	9, 29
Lea, Charlie	7, 36	White, Rondell	28, **28**
Marshall, Mike	7	Wilkerson, Brad	11
Martinez, Dennis	7, 22, 43	Williams, Dick	25, 40, **41**
Martinez, Pedro	**8**, 9, 22, **22**,	Wills, Maury	37
	26, 27, **27**, 38, 40	Young, Dmitri	11, **15**, 40
Mauch, Gene	25, **34**, 39, 40	Zimmerman, Ryan	**10**, 11, 23,
Milledge, Lastings	11		**23**, 36, 38, **38**, 43

The Team

MARK STEWART has written more than 25 books on baseball, and over 100 sports books for kids. He grew up in New York City during the 1960s rooting for the Yankees and Mets, and now takes his two daughters, Mariah and Rachel, to the same ball-parks. Mark comes from a family of writers. His grand-father was Sunday Editor of the *New York Times* and his mother was Articles Editor of *Ladies' Home Journal* and *McCall's*. Mark has profiled hundreds of athletes over the last 20 years. He has also written several books about his native New York and New Jersey, his home today. Mark is a graduate of Duke University, with a degree in history. He lives with his daughters and wife, Sarah, overlooking Sandy Hook, NJ.

JAMES L. GATES, JR. has served as Library Director at the National Baseball Hall of Fame since 1995. He had previously served in academic libraries for almost fifteen years. He holds degrees from Belmont Abbey College, the University of Notre Dame, and Indiana University. During his career Jim has authored several academic articles and has served in an editorial capacity on multiple book, magazine, and museum publications, and he also serves as host for the Annual Cooperstown Symposium on Baseball and American Culture. He is an ardent Baltimore Orioles fan and enjoys watching baseball with his wife and two children.